Spiritual Laws for Personal Success

Dr. Olatunji Akintilo

Dedication

This book is dedicated to the world's youth, to those who feel they are left behind in the affairs of this world.

Acknowledgements

That which has been is what will be, that which is done is what will be done, and there is nothing new under the sun.

Ecclesiastes 1:9

This book is a result of years of research into the practical application of biblical principles that can help any individual attain personal prosperity. Inferences are drawn from Bible teaching by several of my teachers, some in person but many remotely through the privilege of technology.

I owe great appreciation to Pastors Jerry and Chris McQuay of Christian Life Center, Tinley Park, Illinois; Pastor Milton Jones of Heritage Baptist Church, Frankfort, Illinois; Apostle K.C. Price of Ever Increasing Faith Church in California; the late Dr. Myles Munroe of Bahamas Faith Ministries, Nassau, Bahamas; and many others. Bill Jurevich of Image Group, Bourbonnais IL provided much needed support and trust. Rob Forster and staff of Media Services, Olivet Nazarene University, Bourbonnais IL made the entire project feasible. I remain grateful to my family for their constant encouragement. To God be the glory for His love for all people and for guiding me in writing this book.

Contents

Foreword

It is a special honor and privilege for me to write the foreword to this book, which sets out so thoroughly and brilliantly the indisputable spiritual laws for personal success based on the truth of the Word of God.

The book is primarily directed to the youth—those who will have more time to put into practice and reap the rewards of studying and applying these laws to their lives. However, these principles are applicable to every person of purpose that desires the wisdom and power for living a fulfilled life in every area.

In this book, the spiritual laws are set forth in steps that are attainable, even in a busy world. The Law of Hearing is where it begins. The Law of the Mind and the Law of Work bring into clear and practical perspective the Law of Vision and the Law of Sowing and Reaping. The Law of Words has creative expressions of faith, and, finally, the Law of Meekness shows the pathway to inherit the earth and do it the right way.

I commend Dr. Olatunji Akintilo, a man of many laudable qualities, for his excellent work. I have known him for many years as he lived out his faith, including the privilege of working alongside him in the medical mission field, where he was applying the spiritual Law of Work.

Reading reflectively through the manuscript was, for me, an experience in self-assessment and positive redirection.

I very highly recommend this book to all those who seek the truth and the wisdom to live a successful and fulfilling life.

Yomi Akintorin, M.D.

Chicago, Illinois, September 2019

Preface

For You have made him a little lower than the angels, And You have crowned him with glory and honor. You have made him to have dominion over the works of Your hands; You have put all things under his feet.

Psalm 8:5–6

As God's love is universal, so is this book written for everyone. Everybody can benefit, particularly the world's youth that feel left behind in the affairs of the world. The common saying refers to those that are compelled to arise from a bare rock, with no support in sight. Many are asked to pull themselves up by their bootstraps when, in fact, they have no boots. And we know that description fits the majority of youths in most African and other third-world countries. The harsh reality affects too many, so much so that finding two square meals per day is an insurmountable challenge. This does not have to be so.

The Bible shows us that all people are born with the potential to succeed in this life. God Almighty has made a provision for all, regardless of birth heritage, race, ethnicity, or geographical location.

And the first prerequisite to achieving such a life is to be clear about self-identity. Next, we need to discover the spiritual laws for personal success that are carefully hidden in the Holy Bible, like golden gems. Some of these laws make common sense, while others leave us in awe. All of them work in our favor a hundred percent of the time. This book examines some of the major spiritual laws in detail. But first, we need to address the critical question of a person's identity: Who are you?

That question is not just about a name. What is being asked is deep-seated in your soul: What do you see as your identity? Many people don't think much of themselves. They look in the mirror and think, *I'm not much!* They think, *I am fat, I am short, I am uneducated, I have a strange accent, I don't have any family support, I am nothing.* This issue of self-identity is so critical because it determines the totality of our lives.

We hear of African leaders who tend to display their own error of self-identity. Whenever they award contracts for local projects, they give the work out to foreign companies. If they get sick, they hop on an airplane and go to foreign countries to seek medical treatment. They ignore the local experts at the local hospitals, universities, and medical colleges to go abroad. What does that mean? It means they don't think much of their own selves. They see no value in their own people, no value in their own identity.

To avoid this terrible error in our lives and to attain our personal potential for success, we need to know who we are as human beings. Otherwise, we end up living below our privileges. Too many people think too little about their identity, and they treat others that look like them just as poorly.

Let's consider this folktale. One day, Mother Chicken was walking along a path and discovered a strange-looking egg by the roadside. As a mother, she had compassion on the egg, so she took it home and put it in her own nest, along with her own eggs, and brooded over the eggs. That egg happened to be an eagle's egg. Eventually all the eggs hatched, and here came an eagle in the company of chickens. This baby eagle always thought he was a chicken, so he lived like one and acted like one. However, he was oddly big among the chickens. One day, an adult eagle flew by. All the chickens ran away and took cover. But the baby eagle was excited, saying, "Wow! What a bird!" Mother Chicken then told him he was actually an eagle and could fly like that too. Initially the baby eagle said, "No, I'm a chicken. I definitely cannot fly like that." Mother Chicken proceeded to tell him the story of how she discovered his egg and took care of him. Then Mother Chicken told the baby eagle if he climbed a little hill nearby and jumped off, he would soon discover his abilities as an eagle. The baby eagle complied. "Wow!" the baby eagle exclaimed. "I can fly! Thanks, Mom!"

That is exactly how it is with anyone who does not know their own identity. The individual may keep living at the bottom of the totem pole when he or she should be at the top. That person may keep living as a beggar when, in fact, they should be the king. The baby eagle discovered his true identity and lived the exciting, winning, kingly life of an eagle afterward.

It's the same with us. If we don't know our own identity and if we don't know who we are, we will live far below our privileges. We will think and live failure when our lives should be a resounding success. So who are you?

To discover our identity as humans, we need to go to the Bible. In Genesis chapter 1, we find that God created the heavens and the earth. On Day 1, God created light. On Day 2, He created the skies. On Day 3, He separated the land from the waters and created plants. On Day 4, He created the planets. On Day 5, He created the sea animals and the birds of the air. Finally, on Day 6, He created the land animals and He created man. And as we know, God rested on the seventh day.

In Genesis 1:26, we read, "Then God said, 'Let Us make man in Our image, according to Our likeness; let them have dominion over the fish of the sea, over the birds of the air, and over the cattle, over all the earth and over every creeping thing that creeps on the earth.'" God created man in His own image. We also find in John 4:24 that God is a spirit. And if God is a spirit, then man is a spirit as well. This means man was made of God's quality.

This is man's identity: a spirit that came out of God, made of God material. We are not just skin color, not just nationality, not just tribal heritage, not just the goofy accents; God made man to be like Himself. You and I are made to be like God. Have you ever wondered what God looks like? I challenge you to look in the mirror. Believe it or not, that is God's image.

Genesis chapter 1 tells us that God is a creator, implying that man was made to be a creator too. We see this play out in Genesis 4:17. Cain built a city and named it after his son, Enoch. Imagine man building a city just one generation from Adam. By the seventh generation from Adam, man had invented musical instruments, such as harps and pipes. Man already was working on bronze and iron (Genesis 4:22). Man was created to have limitless creative ability.

Now let's review man's identity as discussed:

- Man was made in the image of God.

- Man is a spirit because God is a spirit.

- Man is of the same quality as God.

- Man was created with limitless creative ability.

Now, God created one species of man. All men are created equal, with the same genetic makeup and with the same abilities, as already outlined. In Genesis 5:1–2 we read, "In the day that God created man, He made him in the likeness of God. He created them male and female, and blessed them and called them Mankind in the day they were created." Man was also created as a tripartite being. Man is a spirit, as we found in John 4:24; he lives in a body and possesses a soul.

A careful study of the Bible reveals that God has made available certain spiritual laws that are designed to benefit all people and to help to meet every material need. This book endeavors to unravel some of these spiritual laws for the personal benefit of the reader and ultimately of nations. It is the author's prayer that God's will may be accomplished in the lives of every reader and of every nation in the world, in Jesus Christ's name, Amen.

Introduction

My son, do not forget my law, but let your heart keep my commands;
For length of days and long life and peace they will add to you.

Proverbs 3:1–2

Those that live in most countries in Africa and other developing nations will agree that the post-colonial leaders have been nothing but a disaster. They have disappointed the citizenry continuously for decades. They are corrupt beyond words. Even the religious leaders are the same. The politicians steal government money; the religious leaders steal tithes. Religion has become part of the problem rather than the solution. Thieves! Thieves everywhere! Hardly any of the leaders are concerned about the youth. And the sad thing is, they are not going to change. Many of the leaders are so powerful and so comfortable in their corruption that…forget it. They will not change.

Now we have come to a critical point in history: The youth of today have to learn to survive and to thrive, regardless of the corrupt politicians, regardless of the corrupt religious leaders, and regardless of the unfair system. But I have good news for you—the same good news that was brought by our Lord Jesus Christ 2,000 years ago.

> The Spirit of the Lord is on me, because he has anointed me to proclaim good news to the poor. He has sent me to proclaim freedom for the prisoners and recovery of sight for the blind, to set the oppressed free, to proclaim the year of the Lord's favor.

> Luke 4:18–19

For the youth of today, I say listen. Stop looking to politicians for help. They will not help you. Stop looking to religious leaders; all they want is your tithe and to control you. Stop looking for corruption to stop; it won't. Start looking to God. Help is available with God Almighty.

This book will reveal to you some spiritual laws that, if put into practice, will transform your life. If done properly, they will guarantee your survival and prosperity. As the popular ad slogan of Nike goes, just do it. Succeed. Thrive. Make it. Then, collectively, the youth can change the system for the better. They can end the corruption that typifies most African countries and other nations as well. God wants to help us, and He will. Pay attention to the discussion on the spiritual laws in the following chapters. Make a mental note of them. Then do them. You have nothing to lose. You will be glad you did.

Simple observation reveals many laws of nature. These laws are statements of the uniformities or regularities in the physical world, things that happen on their own accord or follow a predictable pattern. I invite you to look at some examples:

1.   The law of gravity: Whatever goes up must come down. If a person decides to jump off the top of the Empire State Building without a parachute, that person will make a smash on Fifth Avenue.

2.   Earth's rotation: The earth rotates on its axis every 24 hours, and it also orbits around the sun every 365 ¼ days. The earth simply rotates, and that is done with precision.

3.   States of matter: Water is liquid at a certain temperature range. It turns to solid ice when cooled below a certain point. At another temperature, the same liquid water becomes vapor.

These are unchanging laws of nature. As humans, we don't need to do anything for these events to occur spontaneously on a regular basis.

In the same way, there are key spiritual laws that can be found in the Holy Bible. These laws operate in the spiritual world, which exists and operates concurrently with the physical world. If these spiritual laws are observed, they will produce a guaranteed result, one that translates to things seen in the physical world. The spiritual laws are designed to add value to our individual lives (Proverbs 3:1–2). Let us remember that man was created as a tripartite being. Man is a spirit, he lives in a body, and he possesses a soul (1 Thessalonians 5:23). Man is not limited to operations of the physical but includes the spiritual. The spiritual laws carefully hidden in the Bible include the law of the mind, law of work, law of vision, and law of sowing and reaping, among others. We will examine these laws in detail as we proceed in this book.

Chapter 1

Law of the Mind

For as he thinks in his heart, so is he.

Proverbs 23:7

What Is the Mind?

As humans, we often wonder what the mind is. Where did it come from? Where is it located? Is the mind the same as the brain? These are valid questions that ought to be answered. Everyone should have a clear concept of what the mind is. Have you ever heard the statement, "Have you lost your mind?" To lose one's mind is to lose everything. The individual essentially becomes an invalid, a mere blob of protoplasm, only to be more despised or pitied than admired. And so it is essential to trace the mind to its origin and for everyone to have a clear understanding of what the mind is.

With some research, we find the origin of the mind in the book of Genesis in the Bible (Figure 1).

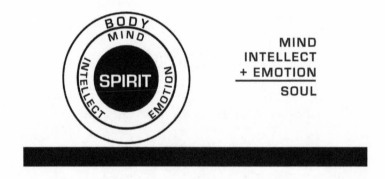

Figure 1

And the LORD God formed man of the dust of the ground (outer circle). He then breathed into his nostrils the breath of life (the two inner circles), then man became a living soul.

Gen 2:7.

The soul as mentioned here represents the spirit and soul combination. The soul proper, separate from the spirit, includes man's intellect, emotions, and mind. Man was given the mind at creation.

Consider this quote from James Allen (1902): "Mind is the Master power that molds and makes, and Man is mind, and evermore he takes The tool of Thought, and, shaping what he wills, brings forth a thousand joys, a thousand ills: He thinks in secret, and it comes to pass: Environment is but his looking-glass."

As mentioned earlier, man was given the mind at creation as a major, major part of our being. According to Genesis 2:7, the human mind is an extension of God's mind. In addition, born-again Christians are guaranteed in 1 Corinthians 2:16 that we have the mind of Christ. We can imagine the mind as our being, only clothed by the flesh. The mind is powerful. By it we determine the totality of our lives, our environment, and our circumstances. Thinking is a tool of the mind. It is erroneously believed you cannot read a man's thought or mind. In actual fact, a man's mind cannot be hidden. The environment is a perfect reflection of what a man's mind consists of. Success or failure, good or bad, individuals as well as nations, our circumstances reflect perfectly the content of our minds. It is similar to the fruit on a tree. Without question, a tree is known by its fruit. Further, our speech portrays our thoughts. As our Lord Jesus mentioned in Matthew 12:34, out of the abundance of the heart (mind), the mouth speaks.

An individual or a nation is poor because that is what has been determined in the mind of the person or the populace. Any poor nation has a majority of people with stinking thinking. Poverty is abnormal and is a choice. Now God is telling the youth, change your mind if you want your environment to change for the better. Don't expect the corrupt leaders to change. They won't. You change. Decide to survive. Decide to thrive, independent of anyone or your government. You can do it.

Consider this poem by an unknown author:

You will be what you will to be;
Let failure find its false consent
In that poor word, 'environment,'
But spirit scorns it, and is free.

It masters time, it conquers space;
It cows that boastful trickster, Chance,
And bids the tyrant Circumstance
Uncrown, and fill a servant's place.

The human Will, that force unseen,
The offspring of a deathless Soul,
Can hew a way to any goal.
Though walls of granite intervene,

Be not inpatient in delay.
But wait as one who understands;

When spirit rises and commands,
The gods are ready to obey.

The Power of the Mind

Let us proceed to examine the powers of the mind. The mind's powers are almost limitless. The Bible tells us in Genesis 2:7 that the human mind is an extension of God's mind, with tremendous creative powers.

The mind is likened to a flower garden. Whether it is cultivated or allowed to run wild will determine whether it brings forth the good fruits by design or bad weeds by ignorance or neglect. A man's thoughts produce character and the totality of his being. Circumstances grow out of thought. The outer world of circumstances molds itself to the inner world of thought, both pleasant and otherwise. Circumstances do not make the man, they reveal him to himself. Likewise, circumstances do not make a nation. They rather reveal the collective thoughts of the populace.

Please note: Man does not get what he wishes and prays for but what he justly earns. Wishes and prayers are gratified when they harmonize with his thoughts and actions. In Mark 11:23, our Lord Jesus

Christ teaches that whoever says to a mountain to be removed and be cast into the sea and does not doubt in his mind will have whatever he says. The mountain moving into the sea is a word picture of influencing impossible external circumstances. And it can be accomplished first in the mind. External circumstances are only an effect. Fighting corruption and poverty in a nation is only fighting an effect. The issue has to be addressed in the peoples' minds first.

Something is wrong in the mind for corruption to take root, whether conscious or otherwise. If a man can radically alter his thoughts, he will be astonished at the rapid transformation it will effect in the material conditions of his life. If the people in a nation buried in the muck of corruption can change their minds, corruption will become history.

As previously mentioned, people imagine that thoughts can be hidden, but in actual fact, they cannot. Thoughts rapidly crystalize into habits that solidify into circumstances. The body is also the servant of the mind. Disease and health, like circumstances, are rooted in thoughts. Strong, pure thoughts produce a healthy body. Thoughts of fear are known to kill faster than a bullet. Indulgence in impure thoughts, even if not physically gratified, will sooner or later shatter the nerves. No wonder Jesus Christ mentioned that a man looking at a woman in a lustful way has already committed adultery in his heart. Clean thoughts make clean habits. The mind accomplishes the impossible through divine law.

It is also good to know that whatever any human being can accomplish anywhere in the world can be accomplished by any other person that believes. We Africans can make Africa great if only we have the resolve in our minds to do so. Start with yourself. Start today.

The Purposeful Mind

Thinking is a tool of the mind. To effectively utilize the mind, our thoughts have to be attached to purpose. Until thought is attached to purpose, there is no intelligent accomplishment. As previously mentioned, the mind is like a perpetual motion machine or a flower garden. Left by itself, it will run amok. A garden left unattended will produce unwanted weeds. Aimlessness is a vice, and such drifting must not continue for the person who would steer clear of catastrophe and destruction.

Those that have no central purpose in their life become easy prey to petty worries, fears, troubles, self-pitying, and blaming others, all of which are indications of weakness. These surely lead to failure, unhappiness, and loss.

A man should conceive of a legitimate purpose in his mind and set out to accomplish it. He should make this purpose the centralizing point of his thoughts. The purpose may be in the form of a spiritual ideal, or it may be a worldly object, according to his nature, talents, and inclinations at the time being. He should focus his thoughts upon the object that he has set before him. He should make this purpose his supreme duty and should devote himself to its attainment, not allowing his thoughts to wander away into ephemeral fancies, longings, and imaginings. This is the royal road to self-control and true concentration of thought. Even if he fails again and again, the strength of character gained will be the measure of his true success.

Those who may not have a great purpose should focus on the faultless performance of their current duties, no matter how insignificant their task may appear. In other words, focus on the job at hand. Only in this way can the thoughts be gathered and focused and resolution and energy can be developed. Once this is done, there is nothing that can't be accomplished.

To put away aimlessness and weakness and to begin to think with purpose is to enter the ranks of those strong ones who only recognize failure as one of the pathways to attainment; who make the present conditions serve them; and who think strongly, attempt fearlessly, and accomplish masterfully. Thought allied fearlessly with purpose becomes creative. He who knows this is ready to become something higher and stronger than a mere bundle of wavering thoughts and fluctuating sensations. He who does this has become the conscious and intelligent wielder of his mental powers.

Change Your Mind

Jesus Christ tells us in Mark 1: 15, "The time is fulfilled, and the kingdom of God is at hand. Repent, and believe in the gospel." In other words, Jesus is telling us, "Change your mind."

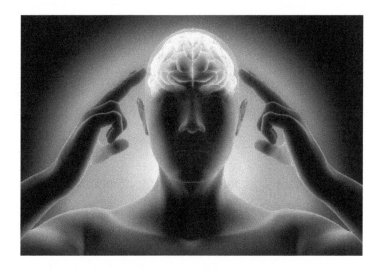

Picture 2

To repent means to change one's mind. Change your mind! Winston Churchill once said, "Those who can't change their mind can't change anything." As was highlighted earlier, the human mind is an extension of God's mind, given to man at creation. Further, born-again Christians have the guarantee of possessing the mind of Christ, as we find in 1 Corinthians 2:16. The human mind is a major portion of our being as humans. The mind determines our environment. Whatever decision is made in the mind will ultimately manifest in the external circumstances.

Fellow Africans, fellow world citizens, if we don't like what we see in our environment and if we don't like our external circumstances, then we need to change our minds. The mind is the determinant of what we eventually see around us. Corruption starts in the mind. Poverty starts in the mind. Societal chaos and lack of order start in the mind. Our thoughts become manifest.

Please, change your mind. Without a change of mind, we cannot change anything. Let's do it for the sake of decency, for the sake of self-respect, for the sake of our unborn children, and for our own sakes as we live day by day. We will soon discover that when we change our minds, our circumstances will change for the better. Posterity will thank us for it, and we ourselves will be glad we did.

How to Change the Mind

The truth of Mr. Churchill's statement is rooted in the scriptures. Proverbs 4:23 states, "Keep your heart with all diligence, For out of it spring the issues of life." As discussed earlier, a person's environment is a mirror image of the content of their mind. Good or bad. Success or failure. Prosperity or poverty. Purity or corruption. They all spring from the mind.

At the beginning of His ministry, our Lord Jesus Christ taught in Mark 1:15b, "Repent, and believe in the gospel." Repent means to change your mind. The youth of today must grasp this astounding truth and the huge implications of the powers of the mind. Whatever change is executed in the mind eventually manifests in the external circumstances. Whatever the mind believes, it can achieve.

If anyone can change their mind, their external circumstances will change accordingly. The mind functions like a building plan, and a firm design in the mind manifests externally with time. The questions for the youth of today are below:

- What would you like to be?
- What would you like to have?
- What would you like to build?

- What position would you like to attain in life?
- What changes would you like to see in your neighborhood?
- What would you like to accomplish in life?

Then change your mind! Imagine your goal in your mind. Be clear. Be concise. Use the power of your imagination. Design the plan. Write it down. Hold on to that plan. Don't doubt it. Then the divine law will start to work for you. Do your part, and the result will naturally follow. You can change your circumstances. You can change your nation. And no one can stop it. It is a spiritual law, so change your mind. Then slowly but surely, you will see the transformation happen in your circumstances. The process may take some time, but it will happen.

We find in Habakkuk 2:2–3 that God told the prophet, "Write the vision and make it plain on tablets, that he may run who reads it. For the vision is yet for an appointed time; But at the end it will speak, and it will not lie. Though it tarries, wait for it; Because it will surely come, It will not tarry."

Surely your goals will be met, your dreams will come true, society will change, and corruption and chaos will be done away with—forever. Change your mind. Change your life. You can do it.

A lot can be accomplished through proper use of the mind. But there are some conditions to be observed to ensure we get the desired results:

1.   Change your mind. That is so paramount it is worth repeating again and again. With a changed mind, the external circumstances will ultimately change accordingly. It is a spiritual law. It is guaranteed.

2.   Don't doubt. Doubt is a goal killer. James 1: 5–8 tells us, "If any of you lacks wisdom, let him ask of God, who gives to all liberally and without reproach, and it will be given to him. But let him ask in faith, with no doubting, for he who doubts is like a wave of the sea driven and tossed by the wind. For let not that man suppose that he will receive anything from the Lord; he is a double-minded man, unstable in all his ways."

Don't doubt. Set your goal in your mind, and then write it down. Don't falter. It will surely come to pass.

3.   Don't be fearful. Fear is negative faith and is a spiritual law by itself. It paralyzes the individual and paralyzes the mind. Even if the feared outcome does not occur, it prevents the desired outcome from manifesting.

4.   Avoid fake religiosity. This is all too common in African cultures. The practice is often one of empty, showy traditions in the name of Christianity as we engage in repetitive prayers. Isaiah 59:1–2 tells us, "Behold, the LORD's hand is not shortened, That it cannot save; Nor His ear heavy, That it cannot hear. But your iniquities have separated you from your God; And your sins have hidden His face from

you, So that He will not hear." Again, Jesus Christ teaches in Matthew 6:7, "And when you pray, do not use vain repetitions as the heathen do. For they think that they will be heard for their many words."

5.   Get ready to work hard. Nothing of value comes easy. In Genesis 2:5, we find that the Lord at first did not cause it to rain on the earth because there was no man to till the ground. This tells us that man was created not only for relationship with God but also for work. Laziness should never be harbored or practiced.

6.   Do right. Yes, do what is right and avoid short-cuts so that with a clear conscience, you may fully enjoy the great results when they come.

7.   Love your neighbor as yourself. Let everything be done out of a motive of love. Do things that benefit you as well as the people around you.

Chapter 2

Law of Work

And every plant of the field before it was in the earth, and every herb of the field before it grew: for the LORD God had not caused it to rain upon the earth, and there was not a man to till the ground.

Genesis 2:5

If any would not work, neither should he eat.

2 Thessalonians 3:10b

God, the creator of the universe, has given us a set of laws to operate for our daily survival. These laws are designed to guarantee our personal success. In the last chapter, we discussed the law of the mind. We will now proceed to focus on the law of work.

It is no news that youth of today are facing the huge problem of societal corruption of government leaders and religious leaders alike. The system is corrupt. The youth are perplexed, wondering what the future holds. But I can declare to the youth today, there is no need for despair. There is hope!

Jesus Christ brought the solution for the problems of this world 2,000 years ago. In Luke 4:18–19, Jesus said, "The Spirit of the Lord is upon me, because he hath anointed me to preach the gospel to the poor; he hath sent me to heal the brokenhearted, to preach deliverance to the captives, and recovering of sight to the blind, to set at liberty them that are bruised, to preach the acceptable year of the Lord." The solution to the problems of today's youth was provided by the Lord Jesus already. Many are in the form of spiritual laws that are available to everyone to use and benefit from. Yes, everyone can lead a fulfilling and successful life! That is God's plan for everyone on this planet. That is God's plan for the world's youth. That is the way to end corruption in the world.

Genesis 1 reveals to us that God created the heavens and the earth. As part of creation, God also created the laws of nature. The Bible tells us in Colossians 1:16 (KJV), "For by him were all things created, that are in heaven, and that are in earth, visible and invisible, whether they be thrones, or dominions, or principalities, or powers: all things were created by him, and for him."

Further, Psalm 24:1 declares that the earth, its fullness, and its systems of influence belong to God. These systems of influence are invisible and underly the visible events. The invisible systems include the natural and spiritual laws. Gravity, for example, is a natural law and is invisible. The laws of thermodynamics are natural laws and are invisible as well. We cannot see the laws themselves, but we see the effects. If we cooperate with these laws, we get a specific result. Why? Because the laws operate in a specific and predictable pattern. The results are reproducible and precise. They are designed for man's benefit. What goes up must come down. Period.

To review, the spiritual laws for personal success are carefully hidden in the Holy Bible like golden gems. Some are common sense, while others leave us in awe. All of them work a hundred percent of the time. These laws are designed for man, for you. They are designed for youth to be productive, successful, and empowered to put an end to the evil of corruption that exists in the world today.

Back to the law of work. Contrary to what might be popular, work is not punishment. Work is a spiritual law. The Bible tells us in John 4:24 that God is a Spirit. And the first time we encounter God, in Genesis 1:1, we find him working: "In the beginning God created the heavens and the earth." We found a spiritual being, God Almighty, being introduced for the first time with Him engaged in work. As a matter of fact, man is a product of God's work. These facts help confirm work as spiritual and authenticate the origin of work as God Himself.

No wonder we are told in Genesis 2:5, "And every plant of the field before it was in the earth, and every herb of the field before it grew: for the LORD God had not caused it to rain upon the earth, and there was not a man to till the ground." Before man was created, God did not allow it to rain on the earth, because there was no man to till the ground. Eventually, man was created on Day 6 of creation. "And the LORD God took the man, and put him into the garden of Eden to dress it and to keep it," (Genesis 2:15).

We know God created man primarily for a relationship with Himself. But equally important, man was also created to work. This was a duty assigned to man by God Himself in Genesis 2, and it precedes the Fall of man in the Garden of Eden in Genesis 3. We know work later became a toil because of the Fall, when God pronounced the judgement that "In the sweat of thy face shalt thou eat bread" (Gen. 3:19a). So whoever chooses not to work commits a sin.

Whoever says to the youth that they do not have to work is a deceiver and a liar. Any pastor or any preacher that tells people to just sow seed money and not work is not being truthful. Jesus Christ said in Matthew 18:6, "Whoever causes one of these little ones who believe in Me to sin, it would be better for him if a millstone were hung around his neck, and he were drowned in the depth of the sea."

There is no question; we all must work. Henry Ford once said, "There is joy in work. There is no happiness except in the realization that we have accomplished something."

The question often is, why work? The first benefit of work is simple. Money. When you work, you get paid. In fact, unless it is given as a gift or through an inheritance, the only God-ordained way to make money is to work. According to 2 Thessalonians 3:10, if any will not work, neither should he eat. And in verse 12 of the same chapter, we find, "Now them that are such we command and exhort by our Lord Jesus Christ, that with quietness they work, and eat their own bread." Those that shun work, that is, those that choose to be idle, shall suffer hunger (Prov. 19:15).

However, money is not the only reason to work; otherwise, wealthy people like Bill Gates, Warren Buffett, or Oprah Winfrey would not be working. We know these wonderful people are multi-billionaires with more money than they can spend in their lifetimes. But they still work. Why? Because work has other important benefits.

What are some of those other benefits of work? There is joy in work, and work commands respect. It promotes personal integrity as well. In fact, it promotes national integrity. A person or a nation that works calls the shots. Work provides a channel to produce something without waiting for other folks to finish solving their own problems so they can come over to help solve yours. Sound familiar for Africa? I hate to admit it, but many Africans simply sit around and wait for the white man to do it all. That attitude is wrong.

Work promotes health. People who don't do any work get sick often. It is common knowledge that when people retire, their health often takes a nosedive. Many retire and then die shortly afterward. Self-purpose is also typically discovered through work. A person working is more likely to discover their life's purpose than someone that chooses to sit around idle. Work engages the mind, continually posing a mental challenge. It provides and promotes intellectual stimulation. An idle mind is the devil's workshop, as the saying goes.

Take a look at this classic Yoruba poem by the late J.F. Odunjo in the book series Alawiye in both Yoruba and the English translation.

Ise loogun ise

Mura si se re, ore mi

Ise la fi ndeni giga

Bi a ko ba reni fehin ti

Bi ole laa ri

Bi a ko ba reni gbekele

A te ra mo se ni

Iya re le lowo lowoh

Baba re le lesin lekan

Ti o ba gbojule won

O te tan ni mo so fun o

Apa lara, igunpa ni ye kan

B'aiye be fe o loni

Ti o ba lowo lowoh, won a tun fe o lola

Abi kio wa nipo atata

Aiye a ye o si terin terin

Je ki o deni ti ra ngo

Ko ri bi won tin yin mu si o

Iya mbe fomo ti ko gbon

Ekun mbe fomo ti nsare kiri

Mafowuro sere ore mi

Mura sise ojo nlo

In English:

Work is the antidote for poverty

Work hard and work smart, my friend

Hard and smart work brings success

When there is no one to rely on

It's like we are lazy

When there is no one to trust

We focus more on our work

Your mother might be rich

Your father might own a row of mansions

If you rely on them

In truth, you might be on sinking ground

Families are like the arm, while extended family is like the elbow

If you are loved by the world today

If you are still rich, they will love you tomorrow as well

If you have an esteemed position

You will be honored with laughter

If you unfortunately lose your money or position

They will turn their backs on you

There is suffering for the foolish child

And there is sorrow for the child that has no plan or vision

Don't waste your formative years, my friend

Work hard and plan well now, because time waits for no one

We have established that God created human beings to work. The exact work we choose and the nature of our work are also of divine origin. For example, what makes an individual decide to be a physician, another person to be a DJ, another person to be an engineer, and yet another person to be a police officer, a cook, or a schoolteacher? In Exodus 31:1–5, we find an account of how God equipped the Israelite workers to build the tabernacle: "And the LORD spake unto Moses, saying, See, I have called by name Bezaleel the son of Uri, the son of Hur, of the tribe of Judah: And I have filled him with the spirit of God, in wisdom, and in understanding, and in knowledge, and in all manner of workmanship, to devise cunning works, to work in gold, and in silver, and in brass, and in cutting of stones, to set them, and in carving of timber, to work in all manner of workmanship."

To authenticate God's desire for man to work, He typically calls persons for divine assignments who are busy and engaged in their work. Moses was called for his divine assignment while he was tending sheep for his father-in-law (Exodus 3:1). Joshua was called while a servant of Moses (Exodus 33:11). David was sought out while he was in the fields keeping the sheep (1 Samuel 16:11). Elisha was a farmer actively working on the farm while he was called (1 Kings 19:19_. Jesus Christ called Peter, Andrew, James, and John while they were working in their fishing boats. Then Jesus Christ walked into the tax office to call Mathew to be an apostle. It is interesting to note that the Bible did not say God called anyone out of night vigils or out of showy prayer

24

meetings, fastings, or conventions. It just didn't happen. God called people who were actively engaged in their work, in both the Old and the New Testaments. Jesus Christ said in John 5:17 (NKJV), "My Father has been working until now, and I have been working." Many of today's Christians waste their time looking for freebies and attending convention after convention. In truth, there is no such thing as free coffee. Someone has to work for it; somebody must pay.

The final question is when to retire. Western culture has convinced us that we need to retire at the arbitrary age of 65 (retirement age in the U.S.). I submit to you that there is nothing to support this practice. In actual fact, the official retirement age is being gradually increased in many countries. Why? Because many people are living well into their 70s and 80s, and they continue to be productive. Donald J. Trump, the President of the United States, as of this year (2019) is 73 years old. Hillary Rodham Clinton is 71 years old. Should these amazing individuals be asked to retire? Definitely not.

As Christians, we know there is no biblical basis for retirement. Moses was asked by God to climb up a mountain at the age of 120 years old (Deuteronomy 32:49). A person that is physically fit and mentally competent should be working, regardless of age. Biblical Christians should die in their boots. To refuse to work is to take a big chunk out of the benefits of one's life.

Chapter 3

Law of Vision

Where there is no vision, the people perish.

Proverbs 29:18a

The Bible tells us in Proverbs 29:18 that where there is no vision, the people perish. This statement underscores the importance of vision in our lives. So the first question for us is, what is vision? The late Dr. Myles Munroe, in his book, *The Principles and Power of Vision*, defines vision as the source and hope of life. He states further, "Vision sets you free from the limitations of what the eyes can see and allows you to enter into the liberty of what the heart can feel. It is vision that makes the unseen visible and the unknown possible." From these statements, we can see that there are two components of vision: the physical sight seen with the eyes and the spiritual sight that is seen through the heart. Both are equally important, and both are components of the law of vision. Operating both will yield amazing results. Let us remember that spiritual laws are established by God and will work for us a hundred percent of the time.

A warning is due at this point. This section of our discussion is stepping into the supernatural, metaphysical, or the heebie-jeebies, if you like. But we need not be afraid. We are looking at what God established and documented for us in the Holy Bible. As we find in Deuteronomy 29:29, "The secret things belong unto the LORD our God: but those things which are revealed belong unto us and to our children for ever, that we may do all the words of this law." Also, in Romans 15:4, "For whatsoever things were written aforetime were written for our learning, that we through patience and comfort of the scriptures might have hope."

Now, back to the law of vision. We found that vision can be divided into two categories: the physical sight seen through the eyes and the spiritual sight seen through our hearts. We shall proceed to examine both of them.

Law of Physical Vision

Starting with the law of physical sight, our physical vision, let's review the experience of Jacob and his father-in-law Laban as recorded in Genesis 30:25–43. These two gentlemen struck a deal about how Laban was going to pay Jacob with livestock because Jacob was keeping his father-in-law Laban's flock in Aram at that time. Both parties agreed that the brown, the speckled, and the spotted flock would belong to Jacob. The others would remain Laban's property.

After the deal was made, tricky Laban asked his sons to remove all the brown, speckled, and spotted livestock and carry them far away, about a three-day journey. Jacob was left with the plain, unspotted cattle and no hope of getting paid. Remember that the spotted animals were supposed to be Jacob's payment, and these had all been removed by Laban. Jacob then utilized the law of physical vision, and it worked wonderfully for him.

Jacob went whittling. He collected some tree branches, made spots in them, and placed these at the watering troughs where the animals came to drink and copulate:

> Now Jacob took for himself rods of green poplar and of the almond and chestnut trees, peeled white strips in them, and exposed the white which was in the rods. And the rods which he had peeled, he set before the flocks in the gutters, in the

watering troughs where the flocks came to drink, so that they should conceive when they came to drink. So the flocks conceived before the rods, and the flocks brought forth streaked, speckled, and spotted. Then Jacob separated the lambs, and made the flocks face toward the streaked and all the brown in the flock of Laban; but he put his own flocks by themselves and did not put them with Laban's flock. And it came to pass, whenever the stronger livestock conceived, that Jacob placed the rods before the eyes of the livestock in the gutters, that they might conceive among the rods. But when the flocks were feeble, he did not put them in; so the feebler were Laban's and the stronger Jacob's. Thus the man became exceedingly prosperous, and had large flocks, female and male servants, and camels and donkeys."

Genesis 30:37–43 (NKJV)

We find that Jacob became exceedingly wealthy by putting a spiritual law of vision into practice. It becomes obvious through the passage we just read that if anyone else can do the same, they can get exactly the same result. That is because it is a spiritual law, the law of physical vision. This law was revealed to Jacob in a dream, as recorded in Genesis 31:10–12.

Now, somebody might say that doesn't make any sense. I tell that person, go to the head of the class; you got an "A." You are right! It doesn't make natural sense. But it makes spiritual sense. It makes sense in faith. And it works.

However, a valid question is, how did Jacob come across this idea? Did he just make it up himself? We find the answer in Genesis 31:10–12: "And it happened, at the time when the flocks conceived, that I lifted my eyes and saw in a dream, and behold, the rams which leaped upon the flocks were streaked, speckled, and gray-spotted. Then the Angel of God spoke to me in a dream, saying, 'Jacob.' And I said, 'Here I am.' And He said, 'Lift your eyes now and see, all the rams which leap on the flocks are streaked, speckled, and gray-spotted; for I have seen all that Laban is doing to you.'"

Here we find the law of physical vision as revealed to Jacob by an angel in a dream. Then Jacob went to work. He applied the law and achieved amazing results. He became exceedingly prosperous.

Again, let us remember what the Bible tells us in Deuteronomy 29:29: "The secret things belong to the LORD our God, but those things which are revealed belong to us and to our children forever, that we may do all the words of this law." This law of physical vision was revealed for our benefit. We can and should utilize it so that we can become exceedingly prosperous, just like Jacob did.

Again, it is a spiritual law; it is supernatural. It doesn't make sense! But if it worked for Jacob, it will work for you as well. What is it you are seeking to do? What are you trying to become? What are you trying to manufacture? What are you trying to obtain? Where are you trying to go? You can do it! You can get there. You can achieve it by prayer and by utilizing the spiritual law of physical vision. Those things can and will be yours in Jesus Christ's Name, Amen.

The next question to ask is, how exactly is the law applied? First, determine exactly what is it that you want. Then get a representative picture of the thing, position, status, geographical location, or whatever it may be. Place that picture in your direct sight. Make sure you spend at least 15 minutes per day looking at that picture and thinking about it. Be free to dream of that picture becoming real in your life, and get ready to work for it as Jacob did. Those things will be yours with time.

Do you want to become a medical doctor? Get a picture of a famous physician that you know of. Do you want to achieve a certain status in life? Get a picture of someone already in that position. Do you want to go to the moon? Get a picture of an astronaut. Do you want to write a utility app for cell phones? Do you want to disrupt a particular market as Uber did to the taxi industry? Get the appropriate picture, or make one yourself. Just get a picture! The options are limitless, and it costs you almost nothing. Don't doubt the law. It is established by God, and He will bring it to pass. But you must play your role.

Get ready to work. Get ready to take risks and persevere. You have nothing to lose. Just remember, the law of physical vision was established by righteous Jehovah God. It will not work for errors, and it will not work to commit sin. Apply the law to make yourself better so you can be in a position to bless others. Apply the law to improve society. Apply the law to love your neighbor as yourself. What are you waiting for? Get out of here and get started! I will see you on the other side victory!

Law of Spiritual Vision

Spiritual vision is that which is not visible to the physical eye but firmly established in the soul and seen in its fullest details in the heart or mind.

In *The Principles and Power of Vision*, Munroe states,

The Third-World people are defined as those who either did not or were not allowed to participate in or benefit from the industrial revolution. Many were victims of slavery, indentured servitude, and subjection to imperialist powers. Today, despite the proliferation of achievement of national independence by many of these people, most are still struggling with the reality of economic, technological, political, and social colonialism. The impact of oppression on these people has been devastating. They have experienced the loss of self-worth, self-esteem, self-concept, and a sense of dignity. However, the greatest tragedy of oppression was the destruction of the capacity to dream and have vision. The poison of colonialism is the mindset that things foreign are good, anything local is bad. So why dream? Why have a vision? The result is that many of these nations, even after many years of national independence, are still locked in a time warp of self-defeating behavior.

Let's remember that the Bible says, "Where there is no vision the people perish," (Prov. 29:18). Little wonder then that certain people find themselves locked in the nasty, deplorable conditions so well outlined by Dr. Monroe. Some third-world nations are in near total chaos. Simply put, many African nations are perishing.

But at this point, I declare, "No more! No more! No more! In the name of our Lord Jesus Christ, no more." No more shall anyone on planet Earth be without vision. No more shall the people of third-world nations be hopeless and disillusioned. No more shall the people of Africa live a visionless life. Here is deliverance. Here is the Word. Here is the challenge to everyone. And that includes every African child, the youth, and the mature. For God is not a respecter of persons. As the scripture challenges us, so I challenge you today: Get a vision!

Habakkuk 2:2–3 states, "Then the LORD answered me and said: 'Write the vision and make it plain on tablets, that he may run who reads it. For the vision is yet for an appointed time; But at the end it will speak, and it will not lie. Though it tarries, wait for it; Because it will surely come, it will not tarry.'"

And so I challenge everyone reading this book to get a vision and write it down. Focus on it. Pursue it with all your might. Seek it. Pray for it. Get ready to work hard for it. Though it tarries, wait for it— because it will surely come. It will not tarry.

Jesus Christ tells us in Luke 11:9, "So I say to you, ask, and it will be given to you; seek, and you will find; knock, and it will be opened to you." By doing so, the youth can collectively change the deplorable conditions in our communities and nations for the better. Get a vision.

Again, Dr. Munroe defines vision as the source and hope of life. He states further that "vision sets you free from the limitations of what the eyes can see and allows you to enter into the liberty of what the heart can feel. It is vision that makes the unseen visible and the unknown possible." In other words, our life purpose is wrapped up in a vision. It gives us energy. It gives us hope. It carves out an individual's path of life. It is inevitable to a purposeful life.

A careful search of the scriptures reveals to us that vision comes from God. Vision is a gift from God to man, and vision is available to those that dare ask God for it. The perfect illustration is found in Habakkuk, as mentioned above. The prophet Habakkuk complained to God about societal degradation in Israel during his time.

The prophet cried to God in Habakkuk 1:2–4, "O LORD, how long shall I cry, And You will not hear? Even cry out to You, 'Violence!' And You will not save. Why do You show me iniquity, And cause me to see trouble? For plundering and violence are before me; There is strife, and contention arises. Therefore the law is powerless, And justice never goes forth. For the wicked surround the righteous; Therefore perverse judgment proceeds." Also, in Habakkuk 1:13, the prophet states, "You are of purer eyes than to behold evil, And cannot look on wickedness. Why do You look on those who deal treacherously, And hold Your tongue when the wicked devours a person more righteous than he?"

These verses sound like a lot of African countries of today, right? It's just like saying the same things about Nigeria, Cameroon, South Africa, Congo, Kenya, etc.: "O LORD, how long shall the righteous cry to You about Nigeria and You will not hear? Why do You permit so much injustice in Cameroon and South Africa? The wicked reign in those countries. The murderer walks scot free. Blood is not avenged. There is impunity. Lord, do something."

And this is the Lord's response to the prophet:

Then the LORD answered me and said, Write the vision and make it plain on tablets, that he may run who reads it. For the vision is yet for an appointed time; But at the end it will speak, and it will not lie. Though it tarries, wait for it; Because it will surely come, It will not tarry.

Habakkuk 2:2–3

The Lord God's response to societal degradation is to challenge the prophet to get a vision. This illustration shows us the vision we are talking about is your mental picture of a desired future that you should commit to writing. It is unique to each person. Whatever catches your attention, whatever irritates you that you would like to change is God's vision for you. Vision is based on facts of the past built on current realities and for a desired future. Get a vision. Then write it down.

God Almighty is asking us today to get a vision. Get a vision of what you would like to be, of what you would like to make, of what you would like to build, and of what you would like to change. Get a vision of what you would like your community to be. Get a vision! You can get it through prayer. Be bold to ask God. He gives graciously. As we find in James 1:5, "If any of you lacks wisdom, let him ask of God, who gives to all liberally and without reproach, and it will be given to him." Get a vision.

As mentioned earlier, vision comes from God and is a gift from God to man. Vision is free. Vision is dreaming the most possible dream, and it is available to those that dare ask God for it. George Barna, in his book on vision, asserts that the purpose of vision is to create the future. He further states, "The future is not something that just happens; it is a reality that is created by those strong enough to exert control over their environment. The future is not a done deal waiting for response. The future belongs to God and through Him to those who are driven to shape it."

These facts are clearly seen in the lives of visionaries such as Martin Luther King Jr. of America, Eric Williams of Trinidad and Tobago, Nelson Mandela of South Africa, Winston Churchill of the UK, and Mother Theresa. These visionaries described a future yet unseen. They believed the vision and propagated it. They pursued and worked on the vision. They persevered. And today we live in the future that those visionaries worked tirelessly to attain.

According to Barna, vision can be defined as foresight with insight based on hindsight. Vision looks forward to the future and is based on an awareness of current circumstances while learning from the past. Vision is a clear mental image of a preferred future. It is imparted by God to His servants, the visionaries.

This is how God designs the future: through those He has chosen, based not on a person's righteousness but only by His grace. We do not have to be perfect to receive a vision. In fact, James 1:5 tells us if anyone lacks wisdom, let him ask of God, who gives to all liberally and without reproach, and it will be given to him. You, too, can get a vision for God is no respecter of persons. God wants a better future for every individual and nation. In fact, He designs the future through the impartation of vision to those that believe.

Now I have a question for you. Do you believe God has better plans for your future? He actually does, whether you believe it or not. But I urge you to believe. Ask God for your vision, the path to your desired future. Write it down. Work toward it. Let it be the guiding light to your decisions. Look at it often. Pray for it. And it will surely come to pass.

By so doing, today's youth can collectively change the deplorable conditions in our communities and nations for the better. We can put an end to the corruption that defines many third-world countries of today. Get a vision!

We find in James 4:2 that we have not because we ask not. And we are guaranteed in Ephesians 2:10 that we are God's workmanship, created in Christ Jesus unto good works. From these scriptures it is obvious that every individual desiring to live a meaningful life needs to approach God in prayer and ask for a vision. We need to ask God for this vision that brings divine purpose to our lives. To do this, there is a need to approach God personally, through prayer.

The Apostle Paul asked in Acts 9:6, "Lord, what do You want me to do?" And Paul received an answer right away. For the average person, it may take a few days, weeks, or even months to get clarity on the vision. Staying focused on God helps. There is no magic to fasting, but it helps in this process of catching the vision from God. Some solitude is beneficial. The joyful fact is that everyone that asks receives, if they ask correctly and not out of selfishness. . James 4:2–3 states, "Ye have not, because ye ask not. Ye ask, and receive not, because ye ask amiss, that ye may consume it upon your lusts." If we ask for the vision with a motive to primarily glorify God and secondarily to be of service to other people and to change the society for the better, it shall be given.

Quite often in life we see the privileged few standing on the platform of success. We all know Bill Gates, Warren Buffet, Jeff Bezos, and Oprah Winfrey. These amazing individuals are likened to standing on the platform of success 40 feet high. To an average person, there is a blank wall in front of them, and there is no ladder in sight. You wonder, How did they get up there? When you ask them, they are gracious enough to say "C'mon, you can make it! If I can do it, so can you." Meanwhile, most people simply get frustrated at the bottom of the blank wall while trying to advance up the impossible.

This is where the Holy Bible comes in. God Almighty has broken things down for us into bite-sized pieces. The spiritual laws contained in the Bible are meant to guide every person to their own success, step by step. The law of vision is available to everyone. This is the ladder that is desperately needed to climb up the wall to the platform of success—the Word of the living God.

Ask God for your vision in prayer. And when you catch it, pursue it with everything you've got. Do everything we have discussed so far, but get ready to pay the price. Get ready to persevere. Get ready to work. Remember that the purpose of vision is to create the future. If the desired future can be carefully crafted in the mind, then it is only a matter of time. It shall come to pass.

Chapter 4

Law of Sowing and Reaping

While the earth remains, seedtime and harvest, cold and heat, winter and summer, and day and night shall not cease.

Genesis 8:22

Of the spiritual laws for personal success that we discussed so far, this next one is the trigger to receiving. It is the law of sowing and reaping. It doesn't matter how focused or intense anyone is about applying the other laws: law of the mind, law of work, and law of vision. If you are not sowing anything, you cannot reap anything. If you are not giving, you cannot receive.

God Almighty has incorporated this law, which could also be termed the law of multiplication into nature. Typically, a kernel brings up the corn plant, which grows and bears two ears of corn at harvest time. Each ear of corn has about 700 kernels, totaling 1,400 kernels for each kernel that was sown originally. Imagine getting a 1,400-fold return on your investment! And that is no big deal; farmers experience it all the time. Anyone that wants to reap must sow. Anyone that wants to receive has to give.

In Genesis 8:22, we find, "While the earth remains, seedtime and harvest, cold and heat, winter and summer, and day and night shall not cease." And our Lord Jesus tells us in Luke 6:38, "Give, and it will be given to you: good measure, pressed down, shaken together, and running over will be put into your bosom. For with the same measure that you use, it will be measured back to you."

It may be a surprise for some people, however, that this law will work for anybody and everybody. You do not have to be a Christian to operate the law of sowing and reaping. It is God's promise to every human being, to every descendant of Noah. And that includes you. Sow a seed, water it, tend it, fertilize it, and speak positive over it. All things being equal, sowing results in reaping. Guaranteed.

Now, the seed is not limited to planting, as in farming. It is not limited to animal husbandry. It includes money as well. Yes, that's right.

The seed could be money given to people in need or to a Christian ministry, like the Dandy Way Ministries. If the Lord puts it in your heart to donate and to sow a seed in this ministry, please visit the DONATE page at our website, www.thedandyway.org. Remember, give and it will be given to you: good measure, pressed down, shaken together, and running over shall be put into your bosom.

We will now examine in detail how to sow the seed of money and get a 100-fold return. This discussion is designed for those that believe the Word of God, the Holy Bible. As we go into the details of exactly how to sow and how to receive in general, but regarding money in particular, the intellectuals may want to say, "That doesn't make any sense!" I tell such a person, "You are right. It doesn't make any sense." But it makes faith. And it is meant for those who believe; it is meant for those who have ears to hear.

The foundation scripture is the parable of the sower found in Matthew 13:1–9. Jesus Christ taught us about the sowing of God's Word. The underlying principle is applicable to money as well. In verse 8 of the scripture, we find some of the seed fell on good ground and yielded a crop—some a hundredfold, some sixty, some thirty. I submit to you that the best good ground to sow or invest your money in is the Kingdom of God, that is, in a church or Christian ministry that is genuinely doing Kingdom work. Dandy Way Ministry is a good example. Wherever the Lord leads you to sow in a Christian ministry will yield a crop, up to a hundredfold according to God's Word.

Now, this is how it works. If you sow 1 cent, start confessing that you believe you have received a hundredfold return, according to God's Word in Matthew 13:8. When the one hundredth cent, or $1, arrives, which is over and above what you normally earn, thank God for it, but don't spend it. Sow the $1 again. Believe and confess you have received $100. Repeat the process when you receive the $100, and sow it back, confessing the hundredfold return. Then $10,000 comes. Depending on your faith level, you could start spending or re-sow it again. If you sow a seed of $10,000, the hundredfold return of $1,000,000 is more than enough to get anyone on the path of financial prosperity. Let's remember it took only five rounds of sowing to get from 1 cent to $1 million. Amazing!

As we just discovered, it takes only five steps of sowing and reaping to get from 1 cent to $1 million. Yes, five steps. And the starting point is 1 cent, or its equivalent in any currency. This amount is available to virtually everyone on this planet. Anybody can find 1 cent! Just get a broom and sweep your house. I guarantee you will find 1 cent lurking somewhere. Then sow the money in an offering plate of a church or in a Christian ministry. The principle outlined by our Lord Jesus Christ in the parable of the sower in Matthew 13:3–8 will kick in. In verse 8 of the same chapter, we find, "Still other seed fell on good soil, where it produced a crop – a hundred, sixty or thirty times what was sown" (NIV). Also, in verse 11, Jesus Christ declares that the knowledge of the secrets of the kingdom of heaven has been given to you. It is a divine secret.

The only caveat is that there is no promise of time. We only have the guarantee that it will happen, and it will. And it is not necessary to start at 1 cent, as used in this illustration; you could start with any amount. Just do the hundredfold calculation from there.

Now, let's remember, the principle will only work for those that believe. All things are possible for them that believe. In Mark 9:23, Jesus said, "If you can believe, all things *are* possible to him who believes." In Matthew 17:20 we find that Jesus said to them, "For assuredly, I say to you, if you have faith as a mustard seed, you will say to this mountain, 'Move from here to there,' and it will move; and nothing will be impossible for you.'" If you have faith, you will tell financial prosperity to move into your life, and it will. You will start sowing and reaping and sowing and reaping and will see yourself become exceedingly prosperous. If you have faith, you will say to the plague of corruption in the continent of Africa, move away, and it will move. You will say to the societal degradation that typifies most African countries, disappear, and it will obey you.

Start sowing today. If the Lord leads you to sow into a church or a Christian ministry, don't resist. Go ahead. Whatever you sow will yield a crop, up to a hundredfold return, according to God's Word. But the principle should not be misunderstood as an excuse to dodge work. We all must work. We only apply the spiritual laws while doing everything else under our power, including work. In fact, the rewards of sowing may come in the form of more work—to do and earn more. Money doesn't drop from the sky. The only things that drop from the sky are raindrops and bird droppings. Money comes through an avenue. It could be through a gift or through an opportunity of overtime at work. Whichever way it comes, sowing results in reaping.

A discussion of sowing and reaping will be incomplete without visiting the issue of tithing. To pay tithe or not to pay tithes, that is the question.

In terms of origin, the tithe predates the Law of Moses. Abraham gave tithes to the priest Melchizedek after winning a battle. Then Melchizedek, king of Salem, brought out bread and wine; he was the priest of God Most High. And he blessed him and said, "Blessed be Abram of God Most High, Possessor of heaven and earth; And blessed be God Most High, Who has delivered your enemies into your hand." And Abraham gave him a tithe of all the spoils (Genesis 14:18–20). Likewise, Jacob made a promise to God to pay tithes, as we find in Genesis 28:20–22, Then Jacob made a vow, saying, "If God will be with me, and keep me in this way that I am going, and give me bread to eat and clothing to put on, so that I come back to my father's house in peace, then the LORD shall be my God. And this stone which I have set as a pillar shall be God's house, and of all that You give me I will surely give a tenth to You."

I submit to you that tithing is a spiritual law. It is obvious that Abraham must have learned about tithing prior to him giving the tithe. Abraham must have taught the principle to Isaac, who in turn likely passed the tradition on to Jacob.

The tithe was incorporated into the Law of Moses, which means as New Testament Christians, we do not have to pay tithes, because the Old Testament Law was done away with. Galatians 3:13 states Christ has redeemed us from the curse of the law, having become a curse for us. For New Testament Christians, however, we are encouraged to give sacrificially to God's work (2 Corinthians 8:1–4). But then the Apostle Paul said in relation to giving that "I speak not by commandment, but I am testing the sincerity of your love by the diligence of others" (2 Corinthians 8:8). If a Christian is being blessed by attending a church or helped in life's walk by a ministry, it should be expected that they would give to that church or ministry. Otherwise, such a ministry will soon cease to exist. If a ministry sows spiritual things into your life, it should be no big deal for that ministry to reap of your material blessings.

So the tithe becomes a guide to New Testament giving. As we know, the tithe refers to 10% of our income. Although we are not compelled to pay the tithe, giving 1% or 2 % will hardly qualify as sacrificial, as was encouraged by Paul. The spiritual principle or law of tithing remains unchanged in that it is a trigger to open up the windows of blessings, according to Malachi 3:10: "'Bring all the tithes into the storehouse, That there may be food in My house, And try Me now in this,' Says the LORD of hosts, 'If I will not open for you the windows of heaven And pour out for you *such* blessing That *there will* not *be room* enough *to receive it.*'" Again, there is no question that New Testament Christians don't have to pay the tithe, but the giving of tithes triggers a material blessing. The tithe helps us to meet the New Testament giving requirement but only as a guide, not by compulsion. The Jewish nation pays the tithe religiously, and the blessing they receive is obvious to all.

Chapter 5

Law of Hearing

Take heed what you hear.

Mark 4:24

In Mark 4:24, Jesus Christ tells us, "Take heed what you hear. With the same measure you use, it will be measured to you; and to you who hear, more will be given." Also, in Luke 8:18 we find, "Therefore take heed how you hear. For whoever has, to him more will be given; and whoever does not have, even what he seems to have will be taken from him."

In these verses, our Lord Jesus Christ establishes for us the spiritual law of hearing. *What* we hear and *how* we hear are of paramount importance. Hearing is so critical that it is a major determinant of our material success in this life. And how do we know when a person hears? We know a person is hearing when the message is internalized and retained. First, the individual pays attention, keeps and deliberates over the words, and, if required, obeys. If we are not doing these things for what we hear, we are not hearing. Simply being exposed to the sound waves is not hearing. In fact, the Jewish word to hear and to obey is the same word: Sharma. This means, if we are not obeying, we are not hearing. If we don't listen, retain the words, think about the words, and act if required, we did not hear.

> Take heed what you hear. With the same measure you use, it
> will be measured to you; and to you who hear, more will be
> given. For whoever has, to him more will be given; but
> whoever does not have, even what he has will be taken away
> from him.

Mark 4:24–25

Anyone that wants to be successful in this life must develop the habit of hearing. A person has two ears for a reason. We need to use them. Failure to hear categorizes a person as ignorant, stubborn, moribund, or a castaway. The result is poverty and disease. Please, use your ears.

As we know, hearing is one of the five senses that helps us to understand the world around us. We have the senses of sight, touch, taste, smell, and, of course, hearing. Technically speaking, people can hear sounds at frequencies from about 20 Hz to 20,000 Hz, although we hear best from 1,000 Hz to 5,000 Hz. Sound waves are reflected by the pinna and conducted through the ear canal to the special apparatus inside our ears that includes the eardrum and the cochlea. The sound frequency is then converted to electric signals transmitted to the brain through the hearing nerves for interpretation.

The sense of hearing must be peculiar to be singled out by our Lord Jesus Christ. In Mark 4:24, we are encouraged to be careful about what we hear. In other words, pay attention to the words. How much attention paid to the words determines the utility to an individual. What you squeeze out is what you get. Based on what is obtained from a message, you will put yourself in a position to receive more.

The implications of hearing are amazing—truly awesome. But at the same time, it should be understandable. Everything any individual is ever going to need is already on this planet. Since creation, no single dollar has ever left this planet. All the wealth of Solomon, the richest man that ever lived, or of John Rockefeller, Steve Jobs, Aliko Dangote, Jack Ma, Oprah Winfrey, and every super-rich person that is alive or has ever lived—their wealth is here on this earth. In fact, any wealth of any person, living or dead, stays here on the earth. This earth is loaded with stuff. There is more than enough to go around. Anything any person is ever going to need is already here. According to our Lord Jesus, all we need is information. Listen up! Get information and prosper. Hear and succeed. "Get wisdom, get understanding: forget it not; neither decline from the words of my mouth" (Proverbs 4:5). Matthew 13:9 tell us, "He who has ears to hear, let him hear."

So paramount is our hearing that it is tied with the supernatural. There are nine spiritual gifts outlined by the Apostle Paul in 1 Corinthians 12:7–10: "But the manifestation of the Spirit is given to each one for the profit of all: for to one is given the word of wisdom through the Spirit, to another the word of knowledge through the same Spirit, to another faith by the same Spirit, to another gifts of healings by the same Spirit, to another the working of miracles, to another prophecy, to another discerning of spirits, to another different kinds of tongues, to another the interpretation of tongues." Out of these nine spiritual gifts that are established in the church by God, six of them are speaking gifts. These include word of wisdom, word of knowledge, prophecy, discerning of spirits, different kinds of tongues, and interpretation of tongues. The Scriptures tell us that the gifts were given for the benefit of all Christians.

As in 1 Corinthians 12:7, we find that the manifestation of the Spirit is given to each one for the profit of all, and we note the majority of the spiritual gifts will do nobody any good if there is no one to hear and listen. By paying attention to the words through the spiritual gifts, we are enabled to operate and to receive the supernatural to our benefit. We allow God to work in our lives when we listen to Him and do what He says.

Permit me to issue a warning at this point. These revelations of spiritual laws are by no means meant to encourage laziness. Everyone must work. Pursue education. Pursue professions of your choice. Work hard, and be patient to await the results. We only use the spiritual information as the operating platform, like Windows 10 or iOS, without which a computer or mobile device will be useless. Personal success will be an inevitable outcome of listening and hearing.

As already mentioned, there are nine spiritual gifts outlined by the Apostle Paul in 1 Corinthians chapter 12:7–10. These gifts manifest through the human vessel, that is, through an individual in the context of the church. Six of the nine gifts say something and are designed to benefit every Christian individual. Again, it is interesting to note that the majority of the spiritual gifts just speak. Let us take a look at the six speaking gifts and what they do:

1.   Word of wisdom: This is a supernatural manifestation of the plan, purpose, and mind of God for the future. It is predictive of future events.

2.   Word of knowledge: This gift reveals information about the past or present about persons, places, or things.

3.   Prophecy: This refers to foretelling of future events, as with the Old Testament prophets, or forthtelling of God's Word, as believed in the New Testament age.

4.   Discerning of spirits, not the discerning of evil spirits: It is not the gift of paranoia. This gift reveals the spiritual world. The person through whom the gift manifests may be able to see God as John did on the Isle of Patmos. A person may see Jesus Christ, angels, or demons or even look through and see a man's spirit. Stephen saw through to heaven while being stoned, as outlined in Acts 7:55–56: "But he, being full of the Holy Ghost, looked up steadfastly into heaven, and saw the glory of God, and Jesus standing on the right hand of God, And said, Behold, I see the heavens opened, and the Son of man standing on the right hand of God." Neither John nor Stephen was sleeping when they saw these visions through a manifestation of discerning of spirits.

5.   Diverse kinds of tongues: Separate from praying in tongues, this is a special manifestation or foretelling in an unknown language.

6.   Interpretation of tongues: This interprets what was revealed by the gift of diverse kinds of tongues, and in combination, the two are equivalent to the gift of prophecy.

One quick note: Jesus Christ gave these gifts for the benefit of His Church. Nowhere do the Scriptures say they will stop functioning.

These gifts are in operation today. These gifts are talking. Are we ready to hear?

Chapter 6

Law of Words

Death and life are in the power of the tongue, And those who love it will eat its fruit.

Proverbs 18:21

Of the spiritual laws for personal success that we are discussing, this next one is a biggie. It is the law of speech, law of words, or law of the tongue. Jesus Christ said in Matthew 12:37, "For by your words you will be justified, and by your words you will be condemned." Heavy, heavy, heavy. It is possible to work hard for years on a project or a relationship or to build a super strong structure but destroy it all in just one day by using the wrong words. So we need to take a serious look at the power of words, the use of words, and how to prayerfully avoid a disaster by the wrong use of our words. The Bible tells us, "Death and life are in the power of the tongue, And those who love it will eat its fruit" (Proverbs 18:21). The right words can contribute immensely to personal prosperity, and the wrong words can destroy, big time.

Permit me to give a preface: This segment of our discussion weighs heavily on the supernatural. To the average individual, it probably won't make any sense, but I guarantee you that it makes faith. Our first focus is on the origin of words and languages.

The first time we encounter a written documentation of the use of words is in the Holy Bible. God Almighty used words to create the heavens and the earth. We find words uttered by the Creator with amazing power: "In the beginning God created the heavens and the earth. The earth was without form, and void; and darkness was on the face of the deep. And the Spirit of God was hovering over the face of the waters. Then God said, 'Let there be light'; and there was light" (Genesis 1:1–3). The rest of Genesis chapter 1 gives us a narration of how God used words to create the entire earth and everything on it.

The curious mind may want to ask, what language did God speak in Genesis 1? The answer is, we don't know. The Bible did not reveal it, so we can only speculate that it is likely the same language learned by Adam and the same language that was spoken by all men before the Flood and shortly after the Flood. Then the Flood came, and God spared Noah and his family.

We know that Noah had three children: Shem, Ham, and Japheth (Genesis 10:1). In Genesis 11:1, we find that the descendants of Noah spoke one common language: "And the whole earth was of one language, and of one speech." But we also find in the previous chapter, in Genesis 10:5, that the sons of Japheth had their local languages or tongues that was different from the common language mentioned in Genesis 11:1. The sons of Ham also had their own local languages, as we find in Genesis 10:20, and the sons of Shem had their own local languages or tongues as well (Gen. 10:31). In fact, the Jews believe there were a total of 70 languages among all the sons of Noah.

The common language that everyone spoke was lost at the Tower of Babel, as we find in Genesis 11:6–9: "And the LORD said, 'Indeed the people are one and they all have one language, and this is what they begin to do; now nothing that they propose to do will be withheld from them. Come, let Us go down and there confuse their language, that they may not understand one another's speech.' So the LORD scattered them abroad from there over the face of all the earth, and they ceased building the city. Therefore its name is called Babel, because there the LORD confused the language of all the earth; and from there the LORD scattered them abroad over the face of all the earth."

Again, we can only speculate that among the 70 languages, the only language closest to the original, common language of the world is the Hebrew language. This is primarily because the Shemites were the only family that kept close to God at that time in history. Let us also remember that the original Hebrew of the Old Testament times has been lost. It is not the same as modern-day Hebrew. Similarly, modern-day Greek is not the same as biblical Greek. This should not be a surprise; as we know, languages evolve all the time.

Words are so powerful that God equates Himself with words. In John 1:1, we find, "In the beginning was the Word, and the Word was with God, and the Word was God." If God Almighty can create the entire earth with words, there is no telling what awesome prosperity we humans, who are created in God's image, can create in our own personal lives with the right words.

Our next focus is on the tongues or languages of angels. In 1 Corinthians 13:1, the Holy Spirit reveals through the Apostle Paul, "Though I speak with the tongues of men and of angels, but have not love, I have become sounding brass or a clanging cymbal." Paul is saying here that if he speaks the language of angels without the right motive, it amounts to nothing. So there is a language of angels! And apparently, some people speak the language of angels. We can just take a minute to digest the implication of that. If a human being can communicate directly with the angels, there is no telling the enormity of the outcome. Let us remember that one angel killed 185,000 of the Assyrian army in 2 Kings 19:35. That is one angel. The magicians probably do speak to and commune with angels to accomplish their weird actions. But is this legal? Probably not. Do Christians need to speak the language of angels? Most definitely no.

The language of angels was likely introduced around the time of Noah, when rogue angels infiltrated the human race: "Now it came to pass, when men began to multiply on the face of the earth, and daughters were born to them, that the sons of God saw the daughters of men, that they were beautiful; and they took wives for themselves of all whom they chose. There were giants on the earth in those days, and also afterward, when the sons of God came in to the daughters of men and they bore children to them. Those were the mighty men who were of old, men of renown. Then the LORD saw that the wickedness of man was great in the earth, and that every intent of the thoughts of his heart was only evil continually" (Gen, 6:1–2, 4–5). Jude 6 tells us, "And the angels who did not keep their proper domain but left their own abode, He has reserved in everlasting chains under darkness for the judgment of the great day."

To recap, it is possible for a man to speak the language of angels, but it is likely illegal. That is because the language was introduced by disobedient angels, as we found in the foregoing scriptures, and it only led to wickedness on the earth that was so bad that God decided to wipe out the entire human race.

Now, can Christians talk to and command angels to do things for us? Definitely yes, but we have a better language for the angels, and that is the Word of God, the Holy Bible. In Psalm 103:20, we find written, "Bless the LORD, you His angels, Who excel in strength, who do His word, heeding the voice of His word." We Christians can command angels through God's Word. All we need to do is to speak the Word of God to the angels, and they will obey. That is why serious Bible students stay close to the original versions as much as possible. It is said that the American Standard Bible is closest to the original languages of Hebrew, Aramaic, and Greek. The traditional King James Version is good as well. God's Word has power.

Next we will elaborate on the power of God's Word, the Holy Bible. References are drawn from one Dr. Ivan Panin, an early 19th century Christian Harvard scholar, professor, and mathematician, who once tutored Albert Einstein.

For 50 years, Dr. Ivan Panin devoted 12 to 18 hours a day to the work of scientifically proving the divine inspiration of the Scriptures. If the words of the Bible are of divine origin, then those words have supernatural power. The basis of Dr. Panin's revelation was the ancient Hebrew Old Testament and Greek New Testament scriptures. Both ancient languages use numbers as letters in the written form. Take English for example; imagine words written with numbers (1, 2, 3, etc.) instead of letters (A, B, C, and so on). Looked at as numbers, certain unique numeric patterns of the Holy Scriptures become obvious.

There is a unique pattern of 7s that is noted throughout the Bible. For example in Genesis 1:1 we read, "In the beginning God created the heavens and the earth." The number of Hebrew words in this verse is exactly seven. The number of letters in the seven words is twenty-eight, or four sevens. The three leading words in this verse of seven words are God, heavens, and earth. The number of letters in these three Hebrew words is exactly fourteen, or two sevens. The number of letters in the other four words of the verse is fourteen, or two sevens. The shortest word is in the middle. The number of letters in this word and the word to its left is exactly seven. The number of letters in the middle word and the word to its right is exactly seven. This amazing pattern of 7s is seen throughout the Bible so that it appears the entire Bible is written by one single author, although humanly speaking, the Bible was written by a total of 33 authors.

We can deduce that these words have the unusual pattern of 7s for a reason. This pattern is not found in any other written book in existence. God's Word has power. In fact, it can be said that there is more to the sequence of God's Word than the literal meaning. Jesus Christ said in John 6:63, "The words that I speak to you are spirit, and they are life." God's Words are living words. We also find in James 3:6, "And the tongue is a fire, a world of iniquity. The tongue is so set among our members that it defiles the whole body, and sets on fire the course of nature; and it is set on fire by hell." We are told our tongue or words can control nature itself. In Luke 17:6 we find, "So the Lord said, 'If you have faith as a mustard seed, you can say to this mulberry tree, "Be pulled up by the roots and be planted in the sea," and it would obey you.'"

Jesus Christ is letting us know the power of our words. We can talk to things in nature, and they will obey.

For instance, the Nigerians can say to corruption and moral decadence to depart from the country, and those things will obey. Anyone can command national prosperity, order, and love of neighbors to be the foundation of any nation. All Africans can do exactly that for every African nation. It can be done for every nation on Earth. And it shall be so in Jesus' name, Amen.

We just learned about the tongues or languages of angels and that angels obey the Word of God. We discovered that the words written in the Holy Bible have an amazing pattern of 7s that tells us clearly that it is divinely inspired and full of power. Our words can control the course of nature and nature itself. It's almost scary. Our next focus is on how to apply the power of words for our personal and national success.

Jesus Christ tells us in Matthew 12:36–37, "But I say to you that for every idle word men may speak, they will give account of it in the day of judgment. For by your words you will be justified, and by your words you will be condemned." Again, in Luke 17:6, we read, "And the Lord said, If ye had faith as a grain of mustard seed, ye might say unto this sycamine tree, Be thou plucked up by the root, and be thou planted in the sea; and it should obey you." In the book of James, we find, "And the tongue is a fire, a world of iniquity. The tongue is so set among our members that it defiles the whole body, and sets on fire the course of nature; and it is set on fire by hell" (3:6). In essence, we are finding out that our words can control the course of nature and nature itself.

What do you want from God? What is your vision for your life? What would you like to have? What would you like to be? Where would you like to go? What would you like to accomplish in life? Define your wants, desires, or goals, and write them down. Next, find a scripture that supports your desire; then go to God in prayer with your specific request. From that point, start confessing that you believe you have received what you asked God for in prayer.

Remember the angels do God's Word, as we found in Psalm 103:20: "Bless the LORD, you His angels, Who excel in strength, who do His word, Heeding the voice of His word." Start saying out loud to yourself the scriptures that support what you asked God for, believing God has answered your prayer and that the angels will do His Word.

Let's also remember the essential ingredient to getting our desires granted: the motive of love. Ask God to improve you in this area. Ask to be made a blessing to others. Ask Him to improve conditions for everyone in your family, your community, and your nation. But ask with a motive of love. It may take some time, but those things will manifest in your life in Jesus Christ's Name, Amen.

In Matthew 5:43–45, Jesus said, "'You have heard that it was said, "You shall love your neighbor and hate your enemy." But I say to you, love your enemies, bless those who curse you, do good to those who hate you, and pray for those who spitefully use you and persecute you, that you may be sons of your Father in heaven; for He makes His sun rise on the evil and on the good, and sends rain on the just and on the unjust.'"

Make sure you curse no one and avoid sin.

Chapter 7

Law of Meekness

Blessed are the meek, for they shall inherit the earth.

Matthew 5:5

There are two aspects of meekness: humility and respect for authority. Neither of these comes naturally to most people. In fact, it appears to be part of our fallen nature to be the exact opposite. We are often prideful instead of meek. We disrespect authority in the guise of "doing our own thing." In Psalm 37:11 we find, "But the meek shall inherit the earth; and shall delight themselves in the abundance of peace." The Lord Jesus also made the same declaration regarding meekness in the Sermon on the Mount: "Blessed are the meek, for they shall inherit the earth" (Matthew 5:5). It is simple. Be meek, and inherit the earth. Have peace. We can deduce from the Scriptures that if there is no meekness, the individual has to struggle to survive. Meekness contributes to personal prosperity.

The Sermon on the Mount by Jesus Christ was addressed to the disciples and a Jewish audience. The sermon declared several of the laws of His Kingdom. Although the content has special implications to anyone who is saved in Jesus, anybody can apply the principles in their own lives and reap the benefits.

Meekness is a law that predictably produces prosperity and peace. The meek person is gentle and mild in his own cause, not pushy and not unduly aggressive. The meek person looks to God for reward and for vindication, choosing to trust Him in every situation. One can tell who is truly meek by how they respond to unpleasant experiences. Instead of complaining, finding faults, or talking about "fighting to finish," they have learned to keep quiet and take every such issue to God in prayer. They are willing to take steps of reconciliation and to pursue peace.

The Greek word for meek is prahooce, meaning mild and, by implication, humble. But as the saying goes, the person that claims to be an expert on humility is probably not humble. So this chapter is more imploring than teaching. The practical application is available to all.

In order for us to succeed with the least effort, we need to be humble. We need to recognize our own limitations. We also need to realize our dependence on others. We need each other. No one can do it all and live all alone. God did not design the earth to function that way. Everyone contributes their own part. Everyone's part, however miniscule or different, is of equal importance.

That is why it makes a lot of sense to refrain from cursing anyone, even those we perceive as our enemies. Some African cultures are too liberal in cursing, and by that, I don't mean bad words. I mean casting the bad omen on anyone that displeases us. In fact, we cast omens out of pure paranoia sometimes on folks who are simply minding their own business. This practice is wrong. As the blessing of one person has a positive influence on many others, likewise the calamity of the cursed also affects others and may come back to haunt the person that pronounced the curse. What goes around comes around. Bless and curse not, as the Scriptures say.

Respect of authority is a major part of humility. The Bible tells us in 1 Peter 2:13–15a, "Submit yourselves to every ordinance of man for the Lord's sake: whether it be to the king, as supreme; or to governors, as unto them that are sent by him for the punishment of evildoers, and for the praise of them that do well. For so is the will of God." We are implored to submit to every guidance or directive handed down by authority placed over us, be it parents, a supervisor at work, the government of the land, or church leadership. We may want to add that as long as it does not contradict the Word of God, every established law should be obeyed. Every constituted authority is worthy of respect.

Authorities are of God. As we found in 1 Peter 2:14, they are sent by Him. In fact, God is at the top of every authority and hierarchy. To disobey authority at any level is to disobey God. This is not to say that every person that is a leader was sent by God to be blindly obeyed. But the office has been divinely ordained. The citizens of a nation vote to choose the leader, but the office that is filled is ordained by God.

No wonder the Bible further directs us to pray for those in power. First Timothy 2:1–3 states, "I exhort therefore, that, first of all, supplications, prayers, intercessions, and giving of thanks be made for all men; For kings, and for all that are in authority; that we may lead a quiet and peaceable life in all godliness and honesty. For this is good and acceptable in the sight of God our Saviour."

One more thing to constantly keep in mind is the fact that God owns the earth. Psalm 24:1 tells us, "The earth is the LORD's, and the fullness thereof; the world, and they that dwell therein." The earth can be looked at in business terms as Earth, Inc.; and God Almighty as the Owner. God established the Earth entity at creation and gave us humans the opportunity to develop it. Like the workers in a factory going in for a shift, we all enter this factory to perform our assigned roles. We come with nothing. When the time is up, just like at the end of the shift for the factory worker, we leave. One way. We leave with nothing.

> And [Job] said, "Naked came I out of my mother's womb, and naked shall I return thither: the LORD gave and the LORD hath taken away; blessed be the name of the LORD."

Job 1:21

Let us conclude with this passage from Ecclesiastes 3:9–11 (NKJV):

> What profit has the worker from that in which he labors? I have seen the God-given task with which the sons of men are to be occupied. He has made everything beautiful in its time. Also He has put eternity in their hearts, Except that no one can find out the work that God does from beginning to end.

Since God has sent each individual to this earth to accomplish a task, we might as well make the best use of the opportunity. We should endeavor to operate the spiritual laws, be prosperous, have peace, and make a difference that benefits somebody else because when the time is up, everything has to be left behind for the next generation. And God Almighty remains the owner of Earth, Inc. forever.

Chapter 8

A Call to Salvation

Do not marvel that I said to you, 'You must be born again.'

John 3:7

You must be born again. All the discussion put forth in this book will be meaningless unless you are born again, that is, saved by the Lord Jesus Christ. There is little point to worldly prosperity without eternal security in Jesus. A person can gain a lot of wealth through an application of the spiritual laws carefully outlined in this book. And that's okay. We know a single individual can hardly be of any help to any other person without this world's goods. And that's okay too. But let us remember that all earthly wealth stays here on Earth. No one takes anything to heaven. We came with nothing, and we leave with nothing. Remember that Job said, "Naked I came from my mother's womb, And naked shall I return there. The LORD gave, and the LORD has taken away; Blessed be the name of the LORD" (Job 1:21, NKJV).

Eternity is of utmost importance, much more than any earthly material wealth, and is only guaranteed through salvation into a new life in Jesus Christ, who said, "You must be born again."

In the beginning God created the heavens and the earth. And God said, let us make man in our image, after our likeness. So God created man in his own image, in the image of God created he him; male and female created he them. And God saw everything that he had made, and, behold, it was very good. And the LORD God planted a garden eastward in Eden; and there he put the man whom he had formed. Adam and Eve sinned against God by eating the forbidden fruit. So he drove out the man; and he placed at the east of the garden of Eden Cherubims, and a flaming sword which turned every way, to keep the way of the tree of life.

Excerpts from Genesis chapters 1–3.

Adam and Eve were chased out of God's presence, but God immediately put a plan in place for their restoration. Adam and Eve bore children: Cain, Abel, Seth, and others. Cain killed his brother Abel, but the posterity of Adam and Eve continued to multiply until God decided to wipe out the earth due to the prevalence of evil. God saved Noah and his three sons: Shem, Ham and Japheth. From these three, all the earth has been populated.

According to the Genesis account, Shem and his household stayed close to God, while those of Ham and Japheth did not. Out of the lineage of Shem, God decided to favor Abram, and He made a covenant with him. Abram was then named Abraham by God. Out of Abraham came the Jewish nation.

In the Old Testament, God dealt almost exclusively with the Jewish nation. We see some instances of God dealing with other non-Jewish folks, as in the case of Balaam, but nothing major. That arrangement is temporary; as the Bible tells us, God is not a respecter of persons (Acts 10:34–35). God wants to relate with every person of every nation.

Jesus Christ came as a Jew to deliver humanity from the curse of the original sin of Adam and Eve so all people can get back into God's presence. He came to deliver everyone from the curse of the Law (Galatians 3:13). He paid a great price of crucifixion on a cross. Out of this work of redemption, God, through Jesus Christ, has redeemed all people to Himself. Every person of every nation can accept Jesus Christ as Lord and savior and become a Christian. God also started the Church through Jesus Christ.

As we find in Mathew 16:18, Jesus said, "And I say also unto thee, That thou art Peter, and upon this rock I will build my church; and the gates of hell shall not prevail against it." We find that the Church is established as a new race under God's recognition. We read in 1 Corinthians 10:32, "Give none offence, neither to the Jews, nor to the Gentiles, nor to the church of God." The foregoing scripture reveals to us that there are three races recognized by God: the Jews, the Gentiles, and the Church of God. There are no Whites, no Blacks, no Asians, or any other race as far as the Bible is concerned. Apparently, God does not reckon with skin color. A person's skin color means nothing as far as God is concerned. In other words, no one can give skin color as an excuse for failure. Whatever one person can do; any other person of any color can do as well. That is in God's purview. Wonderful!

We find in Ephesians 2 that God no longer deals with the Jewish nation exclusively but now deals with all nations through the Church. Jesus Christ established the Church, as noted earlier, and every human being in the current New Testament age has the opportunity to approach God personally as an individual. However, each person has to be saved in Christ in order to enjoy this privilege. The person has to belong to the Church race.

Wherefore remember, that ye being in time past Gentiles in the flesh, who are called Uncircumcision by that which is called the Circumcision in the flesh made by hands; That at that time ye were without Christ, being aliens from the commonwealth of Israel, and strangers from the covenants of promise, having no hope, and without God in the world.

Ephesians 2:11–12 (KJV)

Here, non-Jewish people (Gentiles) were reminded that before Christ, they had no dealings with God, being aliens from the Commonwealth of Israel. Gentiles had no hope; they had no God in this world. Gentiles had nothing. On the contrary, the Jews had regular dealings with God through the covenant of Abraham. The temple was in the midst of Israel, and God dwelt with the nation of Israel.

But now in Christ Jesus ye who sometimes were far off are made nigh by the blood of Christ. For he is our peace, who hath made both one, and hath broken down the middle wall of partition between us; Having abolished in his flesh the enmity, even the law of commandments contained in ordinances; for to make in himself of twain one new man, so making peace.

Ephesians 2:13–15 (KJV)

Both Jews and Gentiles are now merged into this new race, the Church. Each saved person can now approach God personally. This is an awesome deal!

Remember that in Old Testament times, out of the entire nation of Israel and the millions of Israelites who were in a special covenant with God, only one person, the High Priest, could actually go into God's presence and only one day a year. That was the Day of Atonement. One person, one day a year, after killing bulls and rams in sacrifices, could go into the presence of God by entering into the most holy place of the temple. This High Priest knew that he entered at personal risk of death if he had sin in his life.

> For through him we both have access by one Spirit unto the Father. Now therefore ye are no more strangers and foreigners, but fellow citizens with the saints, and of the household of God.
>
> Ephesians 2:18–19

In the present New Testament age, all people, Gentiles included, can now approach God individually 24/7 as a saved Christian. Amazing! What was available just one day in a whole year, to just one person, is now made available to every human being on this planet every hour and every minute of the day. Those who have truly, sincerely confessed Jesus Christ as Lord and Savior can now be reckoned with by God. They can enter into God's presence any time. But please note, the individual has to get saved first. The Bible tells Christians, "Let us therefore come boldly to the throne of grace, that we may obtain mercy and find grace to help in time of need" (Hebrews 4:16).

One may wonder, what is the benefit of direct access to God? We can liken it to having direct access to an earthly power figure, like a king of a region or president of a nation. Let us assume a person has direct access to the U.S. President. If the president says to a person, you can call me, text me, or come to see me in person at the White House any time, there is no telling what the connected individual can do. In fact, the Bible tells us in Daniel 11:32b that the people who know their God will be strong and carry out great exploits. It is like saying that those who know the president personally, those who have direct access to him, will be strong and carry out great projects.

Now imagine getting to know God Almighty personally. Imagine having direct access to the God who owns all things. You will be strong! Spiritually, you will be strong. Physically and health-wise, you will be strong. Financially, emotionally, intellectually, and in every domain of life, you will be strong. Your children will be blessed. Your family will be blessed. Not only that but you will carry out great exploits. It is a wonderful thing to have direct, unhindered access to God.

No wonder then that the keeper of the prison in Philippi asked Paul and Silas in Acts 16:30, "Sirs, what must I do to be saved?" The answer is found in Romans 10: "That if you confess with your mouth the Lord Jesus and believe in your heart that God has raised Him from the dead, you will be saved." It can also be found in John 3:16: "For God so loved the world that He gave His only begotten Son, that whoever believes in Him should not perish but have everlasting life."

A saved person has three major privileges. First, the individual is reconciled to God and can re-enter the Garden of Eden situation from whence Adam and Eve were banned. Second, the person belongs to the Church race with unhindered access to God. Thirdly, every saved person has been granted the gift of eternal life. All of these benefits are freely available to every person on this earth. Jesus Christ already paid the price.

Without question, you must be born again.